YES ! CAN

By Kelli Allen and Jeanna Scheve

cognella
San Diego, CA

First published in the United States of America in 2010 by Cognella, a division of University Readers, Inc.

Trademark Notice: Product or corporate names may be trademarks or registered trademarks, and are used only for identification and explanation without intent to infringe.

14 13 12 11 10   1 2 3 4 5

Printed in the United States of America

ISBN: 978-1-935551-88-1

www.cognella.com 800.200.3908

Contents

Background

"We would be wasting a great opportunity if we failed to use our curriculum as a vehicle for developing values and ethical awareness."
—Thomas Lickona

S O, WHY DID you pick up this manual? Do you want to move your classroom into the 21st century? Are you taking a class? Have you always wanted to differentiate or individualize instruction, but just didn't know how to get started? Bravo! You're ahead of the curve already then and in the right place. However, before we start answering your questions, here are a few questions for you!

- Do I know what my own learning style is?
- Do I know the learning styles of each of my students?
- Do my students know what their learning styles are?
- Do my students have a choice in their work on a daily basis?
- Do I give my students choices based on their learning styles?
- Do I always seek for ways to implement technology into my lessons?

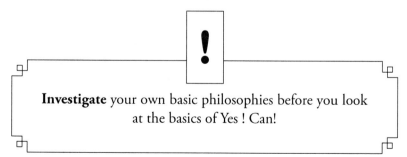

Investigate your own basic philosophies before you look at the basics of Yes ! Can!

Chances are, if you are a beginning teacher, most, but not all, of your answers will be "no". And that's okay, as long as you have two foundational philosophies before even beginning to look at the Yes ! Can learning program:

1. You must fundamentally believe that students in this day and age have the right to have a choice in how they learn.

2. You must understand that to provide choices demands a good work ethic on your part.

"Teachers can change lives with just the right mix of chalk and challenges."
—Joyce A. Meyers

We, Kelli Allen and Jeanna Scheve, are educators with 25+ years of combined teaching experience. In 2004–2005, we were given the challenge to find a way to individualize and personalize the science curriculum for our students. That challenge led us to develop this system of individualized learning plans called "Yes ! Can", which has since been taught to educators of *all disciplines and ages.*

The educational reform that we are currently undergoing involves changing the classroom from one that is teacher-centered to a student-centered environment. The idea that the teacher should be the provider of all knowledge and that the students must simply learn that information in the same way is now being deemed old fashioned and archaic. For many years, educators have known that students all learn by different means, but finally, we are beginning to change the way that we *teach* to encompass these different learning styles.

This generation of students has more available to them at their fingertips than any other generation before them. As a society, we are all reveling in the freedom of choice, the choice to have just about anything tailored to our exact needs and wants. It has happened in everything from fast-food restaurants with "Have it Your Way" campaigns to customized cell phone plans. So, it only makes sense for students to be given choices in how they learn the content by individualizing and personalizing their education.

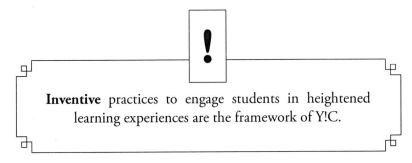

Inventive practices to engage students in heightened learning experiences are the framework of Y!C.

To individualize learning for our students, they were able to *choose* what activities they would like to do to reinforce the content being learned. Meanwhile, the activities utilized current technological applications and were *tailored* to their individual learning styles.

Once the students knew how they learned best, this strategy had a ripple effect. We began to hear our students talk about their other classes in terms of their personal learning styles. They were approaching their other classes equipped with this new tool in knowing what they could do for *themselves* to be successful in other content areas!

We live in a world of customization. Our students' education should be the same way. All of us know that each student learns in a different way, but how do we put that philosophy into an everyday action and integral part of their learning?

The approach of Yes ! Can utilizes the learning style strengths of individual students on a daily basis to ultimately master the indicators at the local, state, and national level. The advantages do not end at just test scores though. Your students will also be practicing indispensable workplace, decision-making, and team-building skills.

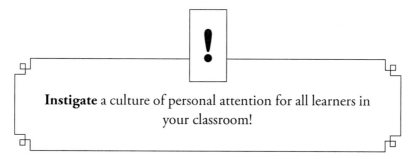

Instigate a culture of personal attention for all learners in your classroom!

The initial Yes ! Can learning plans were used for grades 7-12 science courses with an integrated curriculum (life, earth, and science). In addition, a great deal of choices for the students involved hands-on interaction with technology in various forms. The curriculum was already standards-based and aligned with state and national standards. The Individualized Learning Plans (ILPs) are based on six different learning styles, from which students make project choices within their top two learning styles. As a result of this individualized curriculum, the 2005 State Science Assessment scores were better than ever before at Anderson County High School in Garnett, KS, as they met the State Standard of Excellence in Science for the first time.

"Give a man a fish, and you have fed him for a day.
Teach him how to fish, and he can feed himself for life."

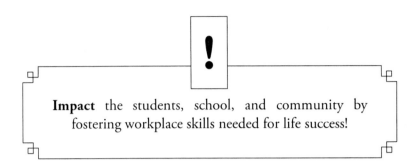

Impact the students, school, and community by fostering workplace skills needed for life success!

The accompanying graph demonstrates the amount of improvement seen on the State Science Assessment from 2003 to 2005 in 10th grade science at Anderson County Jr/Sr High School, and in 2008 to 10th and 11th graders in the same school. The KS Science Assessment was not given in 2004.

ACHS STATE SCIENCE ASSESSMENT

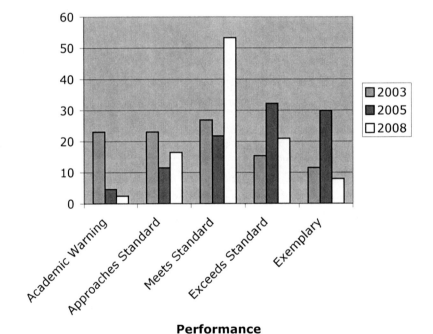

Performance

Now that you have seen the individual categories of mastery for each assessment year for science at Anderson County High School, let us take a look at the total level of mastery from all three years of state science assessments at this school.

BEFORE AND AFTER
DIFFERENTIATION & INDIVIDUALIZATION WITH YES ! CAN

Science Dept. at Anderson County High School

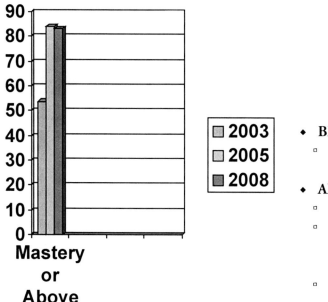

- **BEFORE:**
  - (2003): 53.8% at/meets standard or above
- **AFTER:**
  - 2005: 84%
  - Fall 2007: Multiple standards changed; all but one teacher changed in dept.
  - 2008: 83%

The Yes ! Can learning plan system was implemented at this school in 2004. There was a 30.2% increase in the level of mastery between the 2003 and 2005 state assessments. In the fall of 2007, this high school had a turnover in teachers within this department with only 33% of the original staff remaining. The new teachers were trained on the Yes ! Can learning plan system. As different as each of these teachers were in experience and philosophies, they were able to apply this system in their own unique ways. The system is adaptable on many levels so that instructors can take what currently works for them and expand upon it to offer more individualization and personalization for their students to learn the content. Despite the shift in teachers and a change in *multiple* indicators to be

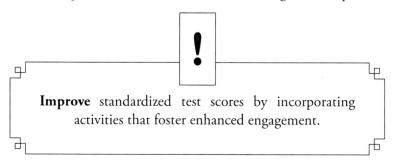

Improve standardized test scores by incorporating activities that foster enhanced engagement.

taught (the KS state board made changes to science standards as late as October of 2007), the 2008 testing results stood strong at 83% at mastery or above, which is a testament to the effectiveness of the Yes ! Can learning plan system.

The Yes ! Can individualized learning system is an innovative teaching practice that differentiates instruction according to the learning styles of students, and does not include the traditional differentiated instruction labels of above-grade level, at-grade level and below-grade level. By incorporating learning style labels, the playing field is leveled for all learners. The opportunity of learning activity choice elicits a high engagement factor, which, in turn, increases student achievement and success.

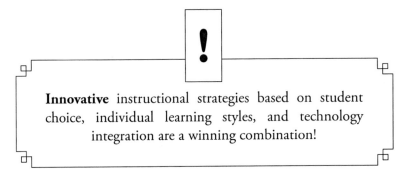

Innovative instructional strategies based on student choice, individual learning styles, and technology integration are a winning combination!

"Whether you believe you can do a thing or not, you are right."
—Henry Ford

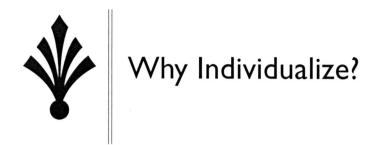

Why Individualize?

"A school should not be a preparation for life. A school should be life."
—Elbert Hubbard

Today's classrooms are extremely diverse entities. Students come into today's classrooms with "unique abilities, backgrounds, learning styles, and interests" and it is the duty of educators to "tailor assignments to suit [their] needs." (Tomlinson, 1999)

To overcome this challenge, teachers must have a strong understanding and desire to make their content approachable for the diverse groups of students. Along with this understanding of the content, teachers must also have a deep understanding of their students. Madeline Hunter once said, "Kids don't care how much you know until they know how much you care." Teachers must recognize and respect the importance of building strong relationships with each student.

There are six fundamental needs of students:

- Voice-the need to express their personal perspective
- Belonging-the need to create individual and group identities
- Choice-the need to examine options and choose a path
- Freedom-the need to take risks and assess effects
- Imagination-the need to create a projected view of self
- Success-the need to demonstrate mastery

—(Clarke & Frazer, 2003)

The Yes ! Can individualized learning system incorporates all of the above fundamental needs of students. Students are allowed a voice in their educational pursuits. Teachers listen to student input and make changes accordingly.

Students gain a greater sense of belonging with the Yes ! Can system due to tailoring activities to their individual learning styles. They also take on new educational identities, such as visual learner, group learner, etc. These identities were not previously identified for the majority of our students.

The freedom to choose which learning activities are carried out is one of the strongest aspects of the program! It has been noted that when students are engaged in something of interest or choice, they are more engaged in the learning process. (Bess 1997; Brandt 1998) Allowing students to have a choice of learning activities empowers them to take responsibility for their learning, versus everyone doing the same learning activity at the same time with few adjustments made for individual differences.

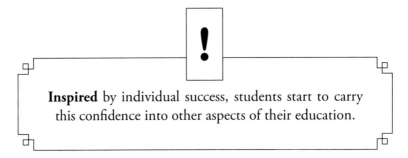

Inspired by individual success, students start to carry this confidence into other aspects of their education.

With the Yes ! Can system, students are able to project a new, positive view of themselves as learners. This success flows into other courses, as the students gain ongoing understanding of how they learn best. The goal of the courses implementing the Yes ! Can system is mastery of the learning objectives as deemed by the state. The student's success toward attaining mastery is tracked and logged as a continual process.

Learning Styles Overview

"It was almost like every minute of every day (I asked myself),
'What can I do to improve myself?'"
—Bruce Jenner

THE THEORY OF multiple intelligences (MI) was developed by Dr. Howard Gardner in 1983. Dr. Gardner proposed that there were eight different intelligences to account for a broader range of student potential. He believed that schools focused primarily on linguistic and logical-mathematical intelligence. The theory of multiple intelligences suggests several other ways in which the material might be presented to facilitate effective learning. (Gardner 1983)

Every child is born with the capabilities to learn. Yet children (and adults) generally have a preferred style in which they learn best. A student may learn through a combination of styles, but usually there is one learning style he or she favors over the others.

For example:

- You may be able to spell by visualizing a word, but your students may not be able to memorize spelling words unless they write them down first.
- Your students may prefer to make a model to demonstrate a concept over writing a description of the concept.

There is no right or wrong learning style. A teacher's primary learning style may be different from their student's learning style(s). For a teacher to work effectively with a student, the teacher will need to understand his or her own learning style as well as that of the student. As a parent, when you identify how your child learns best, you can help them have more positive learning experiences in school.

The following Web sites contain research on learning styles:

- http://www.education.com/reference/article/Ref_Learning_Thinking/
- http://learningstyles.org/
- http://en.wikipedia.org/wiki/Learning_styles
- http://www.learnativity.com/learningstyles.html
- http://www.learning-styles-online.com/

"Nothing happens unless it is first a dream."
—Carl Sandburg

The Yes ! Can system incorporates six different types of learning styles adapted from Gardner's Eight Multiple Intelligences. The following tables are descriptors of the six types of learners the Yes ! Can learning plans employ.

Visual

- Learn by sight, mainly by reading and writing
- Tend to be fast thinkers, gesture while talking, and communicate clearly
- Learn from demonstration—must see it to understand
- Do better with numbers when they see them written

Auditory

- Learn best by listening
- Usually need a quiet place
- Better with numbers when they can hear them spoken
- Has good comprehension when listening to a speaker

Group Learner

- Learn best by interacting with others
- May attend a study group or form one of their own
- First impulse is to socialize instead of finding out what tasks you need to complete—be careful not to miss something

Kinesthetic

- Feeling and touch oriented
- Good at hands-on tasks
- Sensitive to others' feelings
- Learn best by moving and doing
- Has difficulty just sitting for long periods of time

Expressiveness

- Usually does well in speech or writing assignments
- Likes to organize thoughts with study cards, highlighting text, and/or reciting aloud as you study
- Very comfortable with conveying thoughts either by talking or writing

Individual

- Prefer to study on their own
- Work one-on-one with a peer tutor rather than in a study group
- Needs a quiet place
- Class attendance is crucial

Getting Started— 5 Step Implementation

"Step by step, I can't see any other way of accomplishing anything."
—Michael Jordan

STEP 1) INTRODUCE LEARNING STYLES

Choose the multiple learning styles to identify for your individualized system. The Yes ! Can system makes use of six: visual, expressiveness, kinesthetic, auditory, group, and individual. We introduce these learning styles through a Power Point presentation describing each type of learning style to our students after the survey is taken. This introduction is carried out on the first day of school.

For best results, introduce the learning styles as early in the school year as possible. Set the tone and expectations for the individualized instruction setting early on, so the system is not deemed as "something new" that is just being experimented with. The clearer the instructor is with their expectations about the individualized learning system, the more efficient the system will be!

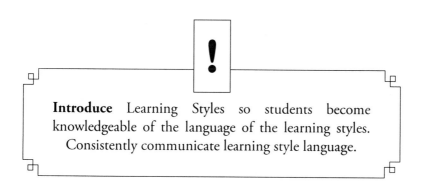

Introduce Learning Styles so students become knowledgeable of the language of the learning styles. Consistently communicate learning style language.

STEP 2) LEARNING STYLE SURVEY

A learning style survey must be conducted to assess what types of learners your students are. Many of the pre-made surveys do not specifically go along with one's grade level or program interest. Check with your school counselor or administrator to see if all incoming students are given a learning style survey, as some schools carry out a school-wide survey.

We recommend generating your own learning style survey that specifically relates to your grade level. We used ideas from a vast array of available online surveys and developed our own. The benefit of developing your own survey is for additional personalization.

One needs to conduct the survey the first few days of school to set the tone for individualization from the beginning of the school year. If one decides to implement an individualized learning program midway through the school year, the survey must still be given to assess how your students learn best.

Make sure the survey identifies the types of learning styles you have decided to incorporate into your individualized classroom. Remind students to take this survey seriously, as it will set the pace for the rest of the year in terms of how they learn best. Give the students ample time to complete the survey to impress the importance of the survey. Get to know your students on a more advanced level by having personal conversations about the results of the survey.

Ask the students if they learn best in accordance to the type of learner the survey identified them as being. For example, "Joe this survey said that you learn best by reading the material, rather than hearing the material. Do you agree with that?" or "Susan, the survey results say you work better in groups than by yourself, do you think that is indicative of your learning style?"

Again, gauge these conversations according to grade level, but be sure to have some sort of personal conversation after the survey has been taken and results have been calculated to ensure the responses of the student.

After working within the identified learning styles for a designated period, if the student feels that they really learn best by other styles other than what was originally identified, then have the student redo the survey and make any necessary adjustments.

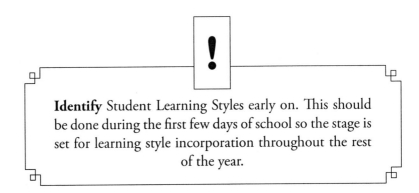

Identify Student Learning Styles early on. This should be done during the first few days of school so the stage is set for learning style incorporation throughout the rest of the year.

Please refer to the learning style survey in this manual for a sample of one to give your students.

Once teachers have assessed the learning styles of their students, it is important to take a strong look at their personal teaching style(s). If the majority of your students are kinesthetic learners, does it make sense to conduct instruction primarily through auditory and visual methods? As instructors, we must ask ourselves these hard questions:

- Are we teaching in the method in which we learn best as educators?
- Are we teaching in the traditional methods in which we were taught?
- Is the majority of our instruction teacher-centered or student-centered?

The Yes ! Can model involves tailoring instruction to each individual student's learning style strength through nontraditional teaching methods that may not correlate with the learning strengths of the teacher.

STEP 3) LEARNING PLAN DEVELOPMENT

This is the most time-consuming aspect of the Y!C program. The individual learning plans have to be aligned with your state standards, indicators, district learning goals and objectives, etc.

If the curricular material does not align with the state standard or indicator, then it is not used.

Each ILP covers a particular indicator, or in some cases a group of similar indicators. We call this time frame a unit, so in essence, the unit consists of material pertaining to the particular indicator(s). The initial plan development is lengthy, but once you have the draft made, in the future, you can make adjustments as needed.

These plans are simple Microsoft Word documents that you can easily create and modify when needed. Remember to include at least *two* activities for each learning style. The minimum of two activities must be included to ensure the student has a choice. By allowing the students to choose the activity, they take more ownership in completing the activity and doing a respectable job on the activity, instead of another assignment forced upon them by

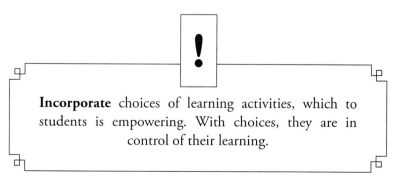

Incorporate choices of learning activities, which to students is empowering. With choices, they are in control of their learning.

the teacher. If working with a team or co-worker, remember to work smarter, not harder; divide and conquer the plans. Have one teacher develop one plan for a specific indicator while the other develops for another indicator. More details on learning plan development appear in the Learning Plan Development section of this manual.

> "Nothing is impossible to the willing mind."
> —Books of Han Dynasty

STEP 4) THE PLAN IN ACTION

If students are motivated to learn the content in a given subject, their achievement in that subject will most likely be good. (Marzano 2003)

This explanation of how the plan works daily is based on a block schedule to give you an idea of how this works. However, for those on a seven-period day, a sample unit plan using ILPs is shown a bit later. Students work out of the learning styles identified at the beginning of the school year. We advise students to work out of the top two learning styles identified. Each day we conduct whole class activities that usually consist of Microsoft PowerPoint lectures, small video clips, whole class review activities such as Jeopardy games, interactive quizzes, etc. The whole group timepiece of the system varies in length. Typical whole group activity times range from 10-20 minutes.

After whole group instruction occurs, students break up and begin their individual learning activities listed on the ILP (individual learning plan). Keep in mind this is a smooth transition.

Provide students with tasks and activities that are inherently engaging. (Marzano 2003) In our experience, students are anxious to start their individual activities and wasted time in the transition from whole group to individual work time is not an issue. Many times students request more individual work time, so wasting that precious time is usually not a problem. They choose what activities they want to do from the list on the ILP.

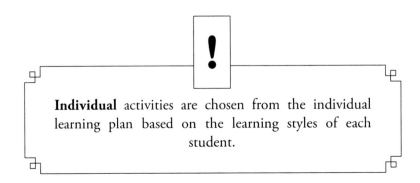

Individual activities are chosen from the individual learning plan based on the learning styles of each student.

Once they complete an activity, they call on the teacher to check their work and at that time the instructor carries out a small question-and-answer session. If the work is completed to the teacher's satisfaction, then the allotted points given will be recorded on the student's ILP. The ILP is the only record of these point values, so it is crucial that the student not lose their ILP.

Once students complete an activity and their work is checked, they quickly go on to the next learning activity. There is no "one and done" mentality with the Yes ! Can individualized learning system. The individual work time is continual with no breaks occurring from the completion of one activity to the start of the next. This practice must be managed effectively by the instructor to ensure that the continual learning activities are taking place by all students.

We provide folders for each student to house their ILP, progress logs, etc. and these documents do not leave the classroom. Provide a structured placement for these folders so students know where to go before each class period starts to retrieve these folders.

Students work on the chosen activities each day during individual work time and are given points for each successfully, completed activity. Rubrics are often provided by the teacher for projects such as posters, videos, skits, etc. (See p. 77—Sample Rubrics for Individual Work.)

The time spent on completing the ILP over the specified indicator varies from unit to unit. The indicators vary in terms of difficulty and complexity, so the time spent on each ILP must also be flexible.

Leave the last ten minutes or so at the end of the class period open for review and/or wrap-up of the day's learning activities. This is a great time for students to share what they learned from carrying out their specific individual activities. This provides crucial feedback to the instructor and serves as an informal assessment opportunity.

Marzano makes the following remarks about student feedback: 1) Feedback should be "corrective" in nature. 2) Feedback should be timely. 3) Feedback should be specific to a criterion. 4) Students can effectively provide some of their own feedback. (Marzano, 2001) The wrap-up/review session encourages students to take their individual activities seriously, since they may have to share what they learned with their peers. This practice emphasizes the importance of the individual work time and increases the accountability of the students.

Variations of this ILP in action can be made based on the instructor's objectives for a particular unit. For example, if more time is needed in a given unit for assessing technical writing (such as a lab report in a science class), then the ILP activities could take place as a review over the unit for a couple of blocks before the exam is given.

Another source of variation may come from having a seven-period day versus a block schedule. In a seven-period schedule, students are in class each day. This example is from an *accelerated* schedule whereby a standard is being covered in five 55-minute class periods.

Monday	Tuesday	Wednesday	Thursday	Friday
Unit Pre-test (15 min.) & PPT/class discussion (35 min.)	Whole group practice (lab, video, think/pair/ share, etc.) (50 min.)	Whole group practice assessment (10 min.) ILP Workday (40 min.)	Whole group review (10 min.) ILP Work (40 min.)	Final Review (10 min.) Wrap-up ILP work (10 min.) Post-test (25-30 min.)

STEP 5) ASSESSMENT

Multiple forms of assessment are carried out throughout each unit. Both informal and formal assessment types are conducted daily during whole group and individual work time. The formal assessments are similar to the state assessment. The question types on the formal assessment are primarily multiple-choice with additional questions as needed. Additional items may be short answer, graphical interpretations, fill-in, essay, etc.

Informal assessment types range from interactive quizzes, teacher-student question-answer sessions, review games, frequent work checks, etc. A wide variety and number of assessments are carried out during each class period. Progress on their formal assessments is tracked on the student's Individual Standard Log, which is discussed in greater detail in a later section.

Through the Yes ! Can learning plan system, assessments are embedded throughout the unit. Assessments are continual and a routine aspect of the course. The formal assessments occur at periodic times throughout the learning plan unit. These are recorded in the assessment table of the ILP. The final assessment carried out at the end of the unit is much like one would normally conduct at the end of a typical teaching sequence. Results from the formal assessments are compiled and used as a tool to direct future course planning. If the overall assessment results are poor, then reteaching of the material must occur in order for the students to master the indicator of study.

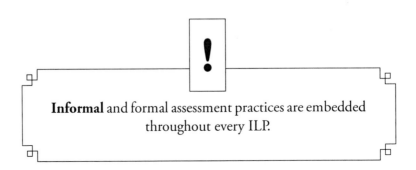

Informal and formal assessment practices are embedded throughout every ILP.

The formal and informal assessment results guide classroom lesson planning, but also provide information alluding to the possible success rate on the state assessments. This informational data is vital to instructors to ensure proper instructional planning for student success and high achievement.

To summarize the integral assessment aspect of Yes ! Can, keep the following points in mind:

- Informal and formal assessments are embedded throughout every ILP.
- Assessments are ongoing and occur during individual work time and wrap-up/review time.
- Project and activity sharing at the end of each class period increases ownership of the learning.
- Formal assessments occur at the end of every unit and mastery is tracked on the Individual Standard Log.

Grading Procedures

"The greatest thing in the world is not so much
where we stand as is what direction we are going."
—Oliver Wendell Holmes

DURING THE UNIT, all activities are graded on the spot and the teacher writes the score on each student's individualized learning plan (ILP). For example, let us say that your class just watched a video and completed questions to go along with that video. You might collect those questions and grade them, or review them in class and have them correct their notes or answers. You may even choose to review each student's work and score it within that class period. Whatever you choose to do, upon completion of this activity, you would move around the room during individual work time and "sign off" on their activity. You only need to write the score and your initials.

The point values for the individual activities should correlate with the time on task of the activities. Some activities are quick to complete and may be only worth ten points. Other activities such as skits, posters, etc. may take more time to complete and thus should be worth, for example, twenty-five points. The time on task should correlate to the point value of the activities.

During individual work time, be sure to monitor that students are working within their top two learning styles. Upon completing all activities within these two columns, students may then choose any assignment from any learning style. This will also help the students in

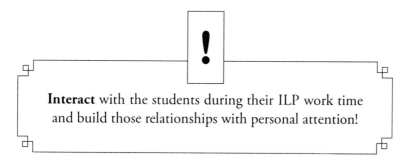

Interact with the students during their ILP work time
and build those relationships with personal attention!

strengthening their weak learning areas. The importance of working within their learning styles cannot be overstated! This is the key to the Yes ! Can advantage! When students are learning the information in ways that best suit them, they are more likely to not only find success on standardized assessments, but to also find success within the class overall. Their recall of information is greatly improved over longer periods of time when compared to those students just choosing from a list of options.

The nature of the individual learning plan is fluid and flexible. One class period you may do a whole group activity, a practice assessment, and then do individual work until the end of the period. The next class period, you may begin with review for the first half and individual work during the last half. You will determine the pace as you go. Remember though, as students are completing work, you must be in continuous motion grading work, answering questions, giving guidance, finding resources, etc. It's a great weight loss program! Rubrics can be developed for PowerPoint, poster, brochure, writing projects, etc. to aid you in grading these during class.

When a student is absent, they will already have the list of what needs to be done upon their return. In sending work home, you may send two or three options from their individual learning styles for them to choose from.

At the end of the unit, you will collect the ILPs and give the assessment. In your grade book, you will need three categories for each unit (each can account for 33% of the total grade). If you are setting up categories on Power Grade, your three categories would be "Whole Group," "Individual Work," and "Assessments."

Now, if your class just finished a unit over the cell, you would enter five assignments in your grade book: "Cell Whole Group," "Cell Individual Work," "Cell Practice Assessments," "Cell Indicator Test," and "Cell Review."

The "Cell Practice Assessments" are any reviews or quizzes that are in the Assessment table of the ILP other than the indicator test itself. The "Cell Review" is a review assignment given to students who do not meet standard on the indicator test. You will not have very many students who need to do this, but for those that do, make the review worth twenty to thirty points, and excuse the assignment for the rest of the students in the class. The review is an opportunity for you and the student to sit down together and review the information covered in the unit, and is one that my students look forward to.

SAMPLE GRADE BOOK VIEW OF ONE UNIT:

Student	Cell Whole Group (50)	Cell Ind. Work (65)	Cell Practice Assessment (20)	Cell Ind. Test(%) (100)	Cell Review (30)
Yhonnie	50	55	18	91	EX
Izaak	50	63	20	97	EX
Christie	40	42	13	78	26

The assessments are practice standardized test questions and there are thirty on each test. Due to the rigor of these tests, students are expected to score at a mastery level that aligns with that of the state in which you are teaching. For Kansas, the level of mastery is a score of 40% or above (based on the 2008 Kansas State Science Standardized Assessment). If there are thirty questions, then the lowest possible score for mastery is a 12/30. Some teachers, however, prefer that the students are pushed beyond just basic mastery in hopes that they may be challenged to exceed mastery. Some teachers may adjust the score for mastery to 16, 18, or even 20 out of 30, based on their own philosophies. However, remember that these test questions are standards-based and mimic the types of questions found on assessments. Be cautioned that students must be used to these types of questions on a daily basis before a final unit assessment in given and before expectations in scores has risen. It is extremely important that students feel the success they rightly deserve when performing at the mastery level.

The level of mastery for each state is based on the average score for students on that assessment within your state. If 40% is average, then within your grade book, the student should have scores that reflect proficiency. However, a 40% by most grading scales is a failing grade. Therefore, an alternative grading scale based on percentages can be used to correctly depict the level of mastery of your students (see sample that follows).

GRADING SCALE FOR A 30-QUESTION TEST WITH 16/30 BEING THE SCORE FOR MASTERY:

Number Correct	% for Grade Book	Number Correct	% for Grade Book
30	100	15	70
29	99	14	60
28	98	13	56
27	97	12	52
26	96	11	48
25	95	10	44
24	94	9	42
23	93	8	38
22	92	7	34
21	90	6	30
20	87	5	26
19	84	4	22
18	83	3	18
17	82	2	14
16	**80**	1	10

*TIPS FOR GRADING ILPS:

1. Use a red pen or a favorite color of your choosing, as long as students do not regularly use it.
2. Sign your initials by the score.
3. Grade it on the spot! Most instructors can tell by viewing and prompting the student for questions over the activity whether or not the student has mastered the information and/or to what degree that information has been mastered. Don't get in the habit of collecting papers to score them later, as this defeats one of the advantages of Yes ! Can—the students are doing the work and you are not loading up a bag of homework every night! The work of both parties is done in class.
4. When scoring whole group work, score it while students are doing individual work. This way you don't have the whole class sitting and waiting for you to get all the way around before dismissing them to individual work. Simply get them in the habit of putting everything in their folders and taking it all with them to individual work.
5. We do not allow students to take their Individualized Learning Plan home during the unit to work ahead. The reasoning behind this decision is the fact that

not all students have access to the same resources at home. Many of our students do not have access to the Internet at home and do not have the opportunity to work ahead, so we try to even the playing field.

6. Students also have the opportunity to go back and work on old ILPs to earn additional points to raise their class grade. This work may be done before and after school or during lunch or homeroom/seminar periods.

We provide an open-door policy, during times available for all students like seminar or homeroom, for students to come to our rooms to carry out and complete learning activities to earn additional points to achieve the desired grade of the student.

SAMPLE DATA

Below is a graph of the results from the cell unit in 2006. We use the same terminology as the state assessment. This assists in the understanding of the adjectives used to describe success on the state assessment and aids in the familiarization of the language incorporated into the assessment.

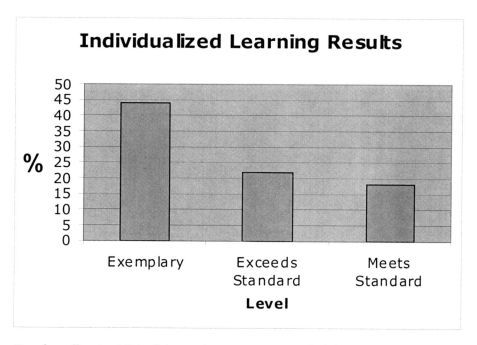

- For the cell unit, 84% of the students met or exceeded the standard. This is the type of data students are striving toward for success for the particular class and on the state assessment.
- In 2005–06, 2006–07, 2007–08, 99% of the "Yes ! Can" students passed science.

- For the 1% that did not pass science, the failure was mainly caused by chronic poor attendance (truancy) and/or failure to make up work after being absent.

"You must have long range goals to keep you from being
frustrated by short range failures."
—Charles C. Noble

Creating Individual Learning Plans

"Goals are dreams with a deadline."
—Brian Trac

THE ILP NEEDS to include a space for the student's name, learning styles, state and/or national standards embedded at the top of the document. The ILP needs to include whole group instruction activities, individual learning activities aligned to the various learning styles, and the assessment pieces.

The whole group instruction pieces are the normal whole group learning activities one normally carries out to convey the overall learning goals. The assessment pieces are the common methods teachers use to assess learning of the concepts. The challenge in developing ILPs comes in incorporating the variety and number of learning activities that are also aligned to the six different learning styles.

A variety of activities are incorporated into the Individual Learning Plans. The amounts of time to create a quality plan is immense, but once you have a quality plan in place, you will be able to use the plan indefinitely with only minor changes to be made. The more direction included into the plan alleviates extensive explanation during individual work time. For example, include where worksheets, videos, lab materials, etc. are found. Make sure all the Web links work and that ample equipment and supplies are readily available. This will save teacher frustration in repeating the same instruction to multiple groups during the same class period.

At least two activities per learning style must be included for the students to have a choice of activities. We recommend more than just two options, but a minimum of two must be incorporated for students to be able to have a choice of activities. On the next page, are sample activities for each type of learner. This is in no way a comprehensive list, but one that continues to grow and change as teachers develop ILPs.

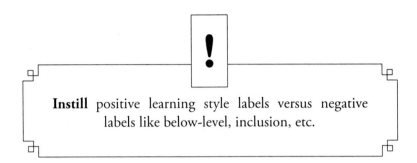

Instill positive learning style labels versus negative labels like below-level, inclusion, etc.

SAMPLE ACTIVITIES FOR EACH TYPE OF LEARNER

Visual	Auditory	Group	Kinesthetic	Expressive	Individual
Video	Debate	Skit	Poster	Poem	Worksheets
Bulletin Board	Podcast	Mini-Lab	Manipulatives	Song	Interactive Quiz
Demonstration	Interview	Game	Charades	Rap	Textbook Questions
Display	Simulation With Audio	Student-Created Video	Mini-Lab	Editorial	Crossword Puzzles
Model	Video	iPod Lesson	Demonstration	Creative Writing	Flash Cards
Flash Cards	Partner Q & A	Debate	Storyboard	Newspaper Story	Podcast
Reading	Lecture	Press Conference	Brochure	Advertisement	Internet Lab
Brochure	Audio Version of Books	Role Playing	Foldable	Dance	Collection
Simulation	News Broadcast	Commercial	Interactive Board	Online Discussion Board	Article Reading

RESOURCES FOR INDIVIDUAL PLAN DEVELOPMENT

One of the most time-consuming aspects of the Yes ! Can learning system is development of the individualized learning plans, but if you have access to resources available one can reduce the amount of time looking for the variety of activities to incorporate into the plans.

The following is a list of common sites we have used to access activities for the different learning styles:

- A subscription to www.lessonplanet.com —A small investment that makes a great difference in searching for activities!
- http://www.teachersdomain.org/ —Videos and interactive simulations for all subjects
- http://www.classzone.com —videos, interactive quizzes, virtual labs, etc.
- Glencoe (http://www.glencoe.com) —Resources for all subjects; includes standardized test practice quizzes, interactive practice with crossword puzzles, BrainPop movies, matching, and more!
- Quia.com (http://www.quia.com) —Online quizzes, Jeopardy games, matching, concentration, and flashcards.
- United Streaming Online videos: http://www.unitedstreaming.com; (Subscription required. Blackline masters and teacher keys accompany many videos.)
- Virtual labs are available at: http://www.phschool.com/science/biology_place/ —Go to the Lab Bench and to the BioCoach for activities!
- Hands-on activities are available at: http://www.sciencenetlinks.com/matrix.cfm
- http://dev.nsta.org/ssc/#micro-units

Other useful Web sites for plan development:

- www.starfall.com
- www.netrover.com
- www.PBSkids.org
- http://www.readwritethink.org/materials/flip/
- http://atozteacherstuff.com/pages/336.shtml
- http://www.teflgames.com/msie_synonyms02.htm
- http://www.do2learn.com/games/synonymsantonyms/index.htm
- http://www.education-world.com/alesson/041p339-01.shtml
- http://www.phschool.com/curriculum_support/interactive_constitution/
- http://www.mathgoodies.com/
- Brainpop.com (There are some freebies, but requires a subscription.)
- http://www.pbs.org
- http://www.emints.org/ethemes/index.shtml

TECHNOLOGY INTEGRATION

"President Obama has challenged the nation to turn around low-performing schools, put highly qualified teachers into classrooms, and ensure that student achievement improves. At the core of these reforms is an emphasis on 21st century teaching and learning in which technology is not merely present, but is used in the most effective ways possible." (Devaney, 2009)

The world is becoming more dependent on technology every day. Incorporating technology into a classroom helps prepare students for the future. Students respond better to technology than they do to photocopies. Even if you are not a computer whiz, technology can be incorporated into the classroom.

Here is what Curtis Bonk has to say about technology and individualized instruction in his book *Big Picture*: "Humankind will come to realize that learning customization and personalization is the norm, not the exception. Web 2.0 technologies and learning plans push us toward the creation of personalized learning environments. Learner excitement will heighten when learning style options can be juxtaposed so that students can simultaneously see, hear, feel, and perhaps even taste the learning. Along the way, any resulting learning will be captured in individual learning portfolios." (Tech & Learning, 2009)

With the Yes ! Can Learning Plan System, technology is also incorporated whenever possible. This depends on the resources you have available to you. The technology integration is one of the real "hooks" to the Yes ! Can system. Your students live in a technology-rich world and access to available technology should be provided within the classroom to enhance the subject matter being taught.

New technologies are introduced all the time, and it is the responsibility of the progressive educator to strive to incorporate the technology into their everyday teaching as part of the technological lifestyle of the 21st century. The following list is a sample of the various forms of technology that could be included in everyday activities of the Yes ! Can Learning Plan system.

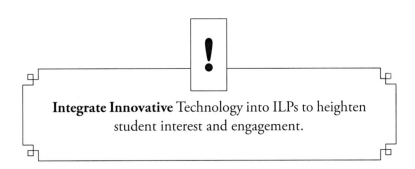

Integrate Innovative Technology into ILPs to heighten student interest and engagement.

TECHNOLOGY INCORPORATION SAMPLES

- Accelerated Reading Activities
- Internet simulations—CDs, internet
- Videos/DVDs—united streaming
- Student-Created Videos
- Interactive quizzes
- Podcasts/Vodcasts
- Probes; temp, pH, force, motion, etc.
- Testing/measuring devices
- Digital cameras
- Video cameras
- Handhelds
- Interactive Write Boards
- Remote Response Systems
- Web Pages; student and teacher created

If you do not have access to numerous forms of technology, the Y!C learning system can work without it, but the integration of technology adds increased interest in the subject matter by enhancing the learning activities through the use of technology.

TECHNOLOGY RESOURCES

There are avenues available for technology acquisition. Check the resources that come with the textbooks. Most current editions of textbooks include CD-ROMs and Web sites with lessons. The teacher's edition textbook includes a list of resources available to teachers. There are also free DVDs and CDs available through textbook companies with sample activities for teachers to view that are interested in purchasing the textbook. We have found numerous virtual labs, simulations, interactive quiz games, etc. With the samples we incorporate into the unit of study, we are under no obligation to purchase the book.

There are also many local, state, and national grants available for numerous funding possibilities. Our advice is to start with a small funding opportunity and then work your way up to larger possibilities.

Grant writing is one method of acquiring various forms of technology. Beware—you must have a specific piece of technology and plan for that particular technology prior to starting the grant. Writing a grant strictly for computers rarely gets funded due to the vagueness of the technology plan.

Most districts also have a technology budget and if educators can document how they will incorporate the technology into their classroom teaching to further enhance student learning, many times the request will get a second look. Too many times teachers ask for a piece of technology because it seems "neat" and have no real plan of action or use in the classroom.

The Internet has a plethora of free interactive quizzes, games, and simulations that also count as technology incorporation. It is the job of the teacher to find the appropriate activities to accompany the learning style for the individualized learning plan.

Ask the computer lab director and other teachers for suggestions. Other teachers may be using programs or techniques in their classes. Some of the younger teachers know more than you think when it comes to teaching with technology. Use their experience to bring technology into your classroom.

So, let us recap how it all plays out at this point. You may have a large arsenal of resources with the Internet or filing cabinets of lessons you have collected and/or created over the years or both. You now have a way to organize all of those resources into something tangible and useful on a daily basis in your classroom. Not only have you identified the learning styles of your students, you are now providing them with a framework from which to choose activities, that best fit their personal learning styles, on a daily basis. You lay the groundwork for the topic in the whole group sessions, which may include PPT presentations, online videos, lecture, whole group discussion, think-pair-share exploratory activities of background knowledge, etc. Then, the students are handed the ILP, from which they can experience and practice the material on an individual level with the power of choice at *their* fingertips. As they are working, you are facilitating, guiding, and monitoring the classroom. As students finish projects, you have a conversation with them, check their work, and sign off points earned accordingly. Daily, you can change the amount of time needed for whole group review, possibly laboratory experience, discussion, and individual work time.

Individual Standard Log

"All things are possible to one who believes."
—Saint Bernard of Clairvaux

THE YES ! Can system incorporates the use of an individual standard log to keep track of the student's progress on mastering the content or learning goals. The student log is a simple word document with the student's name, learning styles, and a list of all the indicators covered throughout the entire course. Each time the student is tested over the specific indicator, their progress is recorded on the log. The Y!C model uses the mastery level that coincides with the state expectation of mastery.

The Individual Standard Log is a great tool for teachers and students to use throughout the school year to chart academic success. The log provides an easy resource for teachers, counselors, and administrators to predict possible state assessment outcomes, course completion percentages and overall student success rates.

The log also provides parents an alternative view of student progress. Too often parents are overwhelmed with grades; whether it be a positive or negative history, grades have been the focus of student education performance. The Individual Standard Log provides an alternative portrayal of student success that often seems a refreshing alternative for parents.

INDIVIDUAL STANDARD LOG SAMPLE

Indicator	Date Assessed	Date Mastered	Indicator	Date Assessed	Date Mastered	Comments
List learning objective identification numbers here	All students will record the date of assessment	Only students who mastered the indicator will record the date here				
(Example) 6.3.1	12/10					
6.3.1	12/13	12/13				

This log is kept in their student folder, which is kept in the classroom at all times. This is the permanent record of the indicators mastered throughout the school year. The goal is for all students to master all indicators.

The teacher determines the definition of "mastery." The Yes ! Can system uses what the state determines as mastery or meeting the standard. We have infused the state assessment vocabulary into the Y!C system for student familiarity and consistency of expectations. At the end of the school year, the log is passed on to the student's future science teacher and the teachers then have an opportunity to discuss each student's mastery of concepts on an individual level.

"It is never too late to be what you might have been."
—George Eliot

Student Work—
Time Management

"I use not only all the brains I have, but all I can borrow."
—Woodrow Wilson

IN ORDER FOR assessment to be valid, it must be varied and done over time. (Wormeli, 2006) Teachers working within the Yes ! Can individualized system of learning check student work during each class period. Rubrics should be developed for use in assessing posters, skits, videos, etc. The use of rubrics speeds up the grading process for these large-scale projects and provides immediate feedback to the students. We give the students a chance to improve on an activity for a better score.

Students keep their work in folders that are kept in the classroom at all times and never leave the room. It is very important for the student ILPs to stay in the classroom, so they do not get lost in the transfer from classroom to backpack, to locker, to home, etc. If the student ILPs are lost, a huge record of points is lost and very hard to retrace.

Remember that the time on task should align with the point value assigned to the individual activities. Allowing students the option to go back on their own and work on the plan to earn additional points is an option for those students who need to earn additional points to raise their grade. This work may be done before or after school, during homeroom, seminar, or even lunch. The teacher's flexibility in assisting with this process will help ensure overall student success. Teachers may use their own discretion for a time frame during which students may make up ILP work to raise their grades. When a student

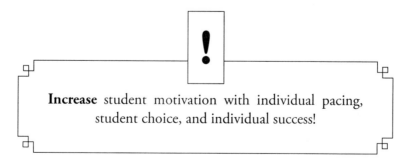

Increase student motivation with individual pacing, student choice, and individual success!

is ready and willing to work, we should allow them to do so, but this is based on a paradigm shift involved in individualizing learning. Quite certainly, a judgment call should be made by the teacher when taking each students case into consideration. Were they legitimately unable to work (computer issues, illness, etc.) or were they not using their work time to the full extent? With constant personal attention from the teacher throughout individual work time, the latter is unlikely, but it may occur.

One method that can be used is to put a cap on the amount of time that work on previous ILPs can be done (one or two weeks after the unit test; at the end of the nine weeks; etc.).

"You can always change your plan, but only if you have one."
—Randy Pausch

Classroom Management

"You have two ears and one mouth.
You need to listen twice as much as you speak."
—Source unknown

AN ADDITIONAL PERK of the Yes! Can individualized learning system is the classroom management aspect. Behavior problems are minimal because students are actively engaged in learning activities throughout the entire class period.

The system is self-paced so teachers are not wasting precious teaching time waiting for the majority of the students to finish one learning activity to begin another. Once students are finished with an activity, the teacher checks the student's work and provides immediate feedback about the quality of the work. Our students were trained to move on to the next activity of their choice to avoid "down time" as we progressed throughout the room to sign off on activities.

Here is what is meant by the statement "students were trained": Students were taught to maintain several classroom expectations during individual work time, not unlike the *procedures* one would have for lining up at the door, signing of hall passes at appropriate times, collection and distribution of work, etc. These were procedures established for individual work time.

The following is a sample of five procedures that have been used for individual work time and most importantly, were practiced each day during the first couple of weeks of class. The teacher led sessions with the students illustrating positive examples of individual work time. Once these were established, minimal reminders were needed for students to remain on task.

INDIVIDUAL WORK TIME

1. **Raise your hand** to signal that you need me.
2. **Show respect** to those working around you by remaining at your workstation and speaking at appropriate levels for the activity.
3. Your project deserves **all of your attention**.
4. **Keep moving forward**. When you finish a project, move on to the next.
5. Need to go get something/go to the bathroom/etc?
   Fill out a planner & just hand it to me. This allows those working to keep working.

Keep in mind that you have given the expectation of students doing continual work, making continual progress. Hold them to that expectation because in real life, their boss will too! In addition, a well-organized plan will assist you and the students in moving through the plan with the greatest level of efficiency. By training students to be self-sufficient, self-directed learners, you have built in the time to work with each student individually, and can provide them with more personal attention.

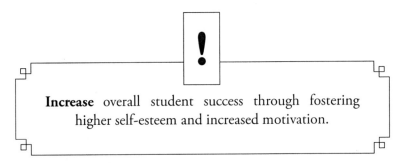

Increase overall student success through fostering higher self-esteem and increased motivation.

Behavior issues are minimal because students are choosing from a variety of interesting, technology-driven, engaging activities that are tailored to how they learn best. Since students are provided the opportunity to choose which activities they want to do, they take new ownership in their educational opportunities. They take on new responsibility to achieve academic success since they are imparted the opportunity of choice.

> "A gem is not polished without rubbing,
> nor a man made perfect without trials."
> —Chinese Proverb

Parent-Teacher Conferences

"Children have never been good at listening to their parents,
but they have never failed to imitate them."
—James Baldwin

THE YES! Can model lends itself to establishing a strong connection to the students, as well as their parents and/or guardians. As soon as you sit down with the parents, you will be able to engage in a conversation about the educational identity of their child, their strengths and weaknesses as a learner, and their decision-making ability as you see it from their use of the ILPs.

By logging student success routinely throughout the school year, the teacher is up to date on where each individual student stands in terms of mastering the content of the course. This information should also be shared with parents to inform them on their child's mastery progress.

There are many character education benefits associated with Y!C Character develops in response to an environment.(Finkel, 1999). The learning environment surrounding the Yes ! Can model implements the character building strategies of strong work ethic, teamwork, self-pacing, organization, time spent on task, and school-to-work interpersonal skills. These skills are modeled and practiced routinely. Sharing these aspects with parents and guardians will be of great value as you communicate the many benefits of the Yes ! Can model.

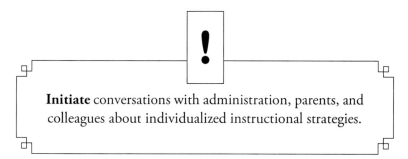

Initiate conversations with administration, parents, and colleagues about individualized instructional strategies.

As one can see, there are many new facets the Yes ! Can learning plan system fosters, such as new educational identities for students, character building strategies and new conversations for parents. All of these aspects are a refreshing change for both parents and students alike.

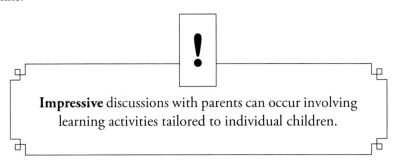

Impressive discussions with parents can occur involving learning activities tailored to individual children.

STUDENT FEEDBACK SURVEYS OF Y!C

A helpful tool during conferences is to invite the students to share in the conversation by using a feedback survey. As we know, students like to share their opinions. However, being asked their opinion of their *own education* is not something that they are used to. So, be prepared for them to stall a bit when you first approach them. Higher achieving students will usually provide very specific feedback, while lower achieving students may need a grid of choices to provide a more accurate response. Feedback can and should be obtained on a regular basis.

A teacher may ask questions like:

- During individual work time, did you choose activities from your top two learning styles?
- Did you study your notes or review individual work thoroughly before taking tests?
- Did you track your own progress for whole group activities, individual work, and indicator tests?
- Did you use the data from tracking your progress to make better decisions on future unit plans?
- Did you use individual work time to the best of your ability, remaining on task at all times?
- Were the projects offered appropriate for your learning style(s)?
- If you could change one thing about the ILPs in the future, what would it be?
- If you could KEEP one thing about the ILPs in the future, what would it be?
- What was your most memorable project in this class?
- Was the class pace too fast, too slow, satisfactory?
- Was the class too technical, too simple, or satisfactory?
- Was the material presented well organized?
- Was the purpose for the lessons made clear to you?

Consider yourself warned: They will be honest! You must prepare yourself to hear the good and the bad. However, this can be powerful data in helping you to see the management of this system through their eyes and make changes as needed.

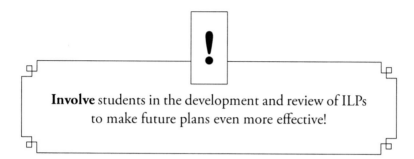

Involve students in the development and review of ILPs to make future plans even more effective!

Testimonials

"Before you can listen to learn, you must first learn to listen."
—Source Unknown

EDUCATOR TESTIMONIALS

The strong points of Y!C., as written voluntarily by conference and class participants:

"With offering the many different choices, there is an ongoing celebration of diversity and I think my students are appreciating the diversity of their peers."

"Immediacy, relevant, & ease of implementation."
—Principal, Elementary, Non-public

"Hands on stuff—that is my style!"

"I am also finding unbridled enthusiasm for the self-selection of activities of my students."

"Teaching to the students' learning styles is a very useful approach."

"This is an awesome idea that I want to try to incorporate."
—Secondary Teacher, Public Schools

"The greatest benefits of this program are not readily apparent with the high achieving student, though I suspect they are there as well, but are more apparent with the marginalized student. For the student with whom reading is a chore, the Y!C program has shown them a way to make text relevant."

"The structure of Yes ! Can is what I've been missing."

"The Yes ! Can model showed us how to individualize the classroom work to fit the student's learning styles! It is great!"

"I will use this in my classroom everyday. I am so excited about the technology integration."

"Individualized activities for different learning styles with a choice of available activities means success for more students.

"You should see my room—it is plastered with student work … I have cartoons, poems, posters galore, a giant word wall, research papers, etc. I had kids coming in to my lunch time to work on their projects (I NEVER got that before). THANK YOU, THANK YOU, THANK YOU! The kids love it!"

Yes ! Can!
I have a plan
To learn
In my learning style

I visually see
What's expressed to me
Through the flashcards
I flash in their pile

I work in a group
I work on my own
I see, I hear, I know

Yes ! Can!
I have a plan
An ILP to help me grow!

By Elizabeth Siegel

STUDENT TESTIMONIALS

Tyler: *"You can do it your way, and there are different ways that it can be done for each person."*

Megan: *"… you figure it out for yourself. … I remember it more because I do more with it."*

Elizabeth: *"We're all learning the same things, but just doing it in different ways."*

Jose: *"You get time … and you get **more** for what you do."*

Jesse: *"We don't have any homework and I have to work after school, so I can't always get work done then."*

Brice: *"You get to work with your own learning style, and it's like an advantage. You get a lot more done."*

Galen: *"In most classes, you read the textbook and (have) fill in the blank answers, but here you actually have to think about it, and you learn it better."*

Devon: *"It's fun!"*

ANONYMOUS ANSWERS FROM Y!C STUDENT SURVEY IN SPRING 2008:

"I was never at the top of my class in points, but it did push me, and I eventually got better at it."

"In years past, I did very well learning with groups and seeing what other people thought and that's how I learned. I liked doing certain activities of my choice that interested me instead of doing something boring."
"I definitely improved my ability to work in a group."

"I want to use the information I learned about my own learning styles in other classrooms."

"I like that this class was challenging and the fact that the teacher always welcomed us to come in if we needed to catch up on any science work! Thanks for always asking our opinion…not a lot of people want to know what high school kids ideas are or what they have to say; it's refreshing to be respected."

"I am not the type of person that can learn with notes and lectures. I only learn by interacting and the class did a great job with that!"

"I feel that in this class I learned more because of the way the lesson plans are set up. I would hope that more teachers would learn this and adjust their classrooms to each kid's specific needs."

"We have a lot of options for individual work, but I want even more!"

"How can a person feel he's a person with dignity and integrity unless someone treats him so? And how can a person feel that he's capable, unless he has some success?"
—Arthur W. Combs

MEASURES OF SUCCESS

The success of the Yes ! Can Individualized Instructional system can be based on a variety of tracking methods. The Individual Standard Log is a valuable tracking method that elicits information pertaining to the mastery of the applied learning objectives and a projection of the success on the state assessment. The overall Pass/Fail Rate of the students working within a Yes ! Can system will also indicate how well these techniques are assisting your students.

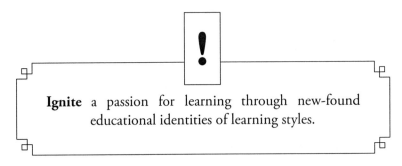

Ignite a passion for learning through new-found educational identities of learning styles.

Of course, much attention is placed on the State Assessment Data, but this should not be the only indicator of success. Since student engagement is increased through the Yes ! Can learning system the number of office referrals should decline. Providing students with a choice of learning activities empowers them so that they feel more in control of their learning. Student Testimonials are also a good indicator of how your implementation of the Yes ! Can model is progressing. Student feedback is valuable and should not be taken lightly.

REPLICATING THE MODEL

To successfully replicate Yes ! Can, one must understand the overall purpose of the model: To individualize instruction to engage students in meaningful learning experiences. The key elements of structure within the model are 1) allowing students choices of learning style activities, which are aligned to individual learning styles and 2) ensuring the activities are student-centered and self-paced for increased individualization.

The essential methods and routines that must be practiced are the daily introductions of learning goals (whole group instruction), and the incorporation of choices of relevant learning activities tailored to personal needs. Wrap-up/review sessions must occur at the end of each class period. Consistent implementation of the methods and routines must occur so the system does not come across as a novelty activity. Finally, there must be expected intrinsic and personalized motivational goals in place on a constant basis.

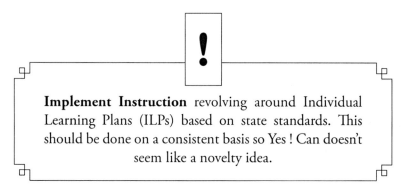

Implement Instruction revolving around Individual Learning Plans (ILPs) based on state standards. This should be done on a consistent basis so Yes ! Can doesn't seem like a novelty idea.

CONCLUSION

The United States is often referred to as the land of opportunity and many educators believe that the United States' public schools are the first step to providing opportunity to today's youth. It can be argued that educators are doing a poor job of providing engaging learning opportunities to their students. Some wonder if educators are leaving students behind, when it is more likely that the students have left the traditional approaches to education behind. In our world of modern times, we are still stuck in an educational system that has been in place since the early 1900s. Students are hungry for rich, meaningful, learning activities that are individually tailored to their own personal preferences. Whether it is using the techniques of the Yes ! Can Individualized Instructional Model or other innovative techniques, it is essential that educators shy away from the traditional methods of teaching and acknowledge and react to the learning styles of today's youth.

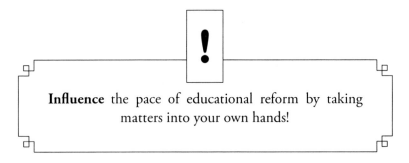

Influence the pace of educational reform by taking matters into your own hands!

GET THE YES ! CAN ADVANTAGE!

!ncrease achievement and !mprove test scores

!ncorporate into any classroom

!mpressive way to !mpact students, school and community

!gnite a passion by !nstilling a new educational !dentity

Resources

"The greatest sign of success for a teacher…is to be able to say, 'The children are now working as if I did not exist.'"
—Maria Montessori

All pages in this section may be reproduced for classroom use.

LEARNING STYLE SURVEY

THE STATEMENTS BELOW describe various methods of learning. Please answer the following questions on a scale of one to four. A four indicates that the statement correlates to how you learn best and a one is least indicative of your learning style.

1.	Making things for my studies helps me to remember what I have learned.	1 2 3 4
2.	When I really want to understand what I have read, I read it softly to myself	1 2 3 4
3.	I get more done when I work alone.	1 2 3 4
4.	I remember what I have read better than what I have heard.	1 2 3 4
5.	When I answer questions, I can say the answer better than writing it.	1 2 3 4
6.	I enjoy joining in on class discussions.	1 2 3 4
7.	I understand math problems when they are written down better than heard.	1 2 3 4
8.	I understand spoken directions better than written ones.	1 2 3 4
9.	I like to work by myself.	1 2 3 4
10.	I would rather show and explain how something works than write about how it works.	1 2 3 4

11. If someone tells me three numbers to add, I usually get the right answer without writing them down.	1 2 3 4
12. I prefer to work with a group than alone.	1 2 3 4
13. A graph or chart is easier for me to understand than hearing the data.	1 2 3 4
14. Writing a spelling word several times helps me to remember it better.	1 2 3 4
15. I learn better if someone reads to me than if I read silently to myself.	1 2 3 4
16. I learn best when I study alone.	1 2 3 4
17. I do my best work in groups.	1 2 3 4
18. In a group project, I would rather make a chart or poster than gather information.	1 2 3 4
19. I remember more of what I learn if I learn it alone.	1 2 3 4
20. I do well in classes where most of the information has to be read.	1 2 3 4
21. If I have to decide something, I ask other people for their opinion.	1 2 3 4
22. I like to make things with my hands.	1 2 3 4
23. I don't mind doing written assignments.	1 2 3 4
24. It is easy for me to tell about the things I know.	1 2 3 4
25. If I understand a problem, I like to help someone else understand it also.	1 2 3 4
26. I enjoy helping others learn while I learn.	1 2 3 4
27. I understand what I have learned better when I am involved in making something.	1 2 3 4
28. The things I write on paper sound better than when I say them.	1 2 3 4
29. I find it easier to remember what I have heard than what I have read.	1 2 3 4
30. It is fun to learn with classmates, but it is hard to study with them.	1 2 3 4

Score Sheet

Visual	Individual	Auditory
4 _____	3 _____	2 _____
7 _____	9 _____	8 _____
13 _____	16 _____	11 _____
14 _____	19 _____	15 _____
20 _____	30 _____	29 _____
Total _____	Total _____	Total _____
Group	Kinesthetic (Hands-On)	Expressive
12 _____	1 _____	5 _____
17 _____	10 _____	6 _____
21 _____	18 _____	23 _____
25 _____	22 _____	24 _____
26 _____	27 _____	28 _____
Total _____	Total _____	Total _____
Highest total identifies your major learning style. Second highest total indicates your minor learning style.	Major Learning Style	Minor Learning Style

LEARNING PLAN BRAINSTORM

Indicator (Learning Goal):_____

Description:

BASELINE ACTIVITIES:

- ♦ What is the most significant information provided from this indicator?
- ♦ In what ways would I like students to cover this information as a whole class?

BASELINE ACTIVITIES FOR WHOLE CLASS:

Activity	Points Earned	Points Possible

REAL WORLD CONNECTIONS:

ASSESSMENT:

Review the information covered in the baseline activities to choose an appropriate assessment.

- ♦ How will my students review for the assessment?
- ♦ How will my students be assessed?

Activity	Points Earned	Points Possible

WHEN PLANNING INDIVIDUAL ACTIVITIES:

Keep In Mind:

1. What indicators or units are the most challenging for my students?
2. What activities do I ALREADY use? In which learning style(s) would those activities work?
3. What technologies do I have available and how can I integrate technology throughout the plan?

Grade Level	Elementary	Middle	High
Visual			
Auditory			
Group			
Kinesthetic			
Expressiveness			
Individual			

BLANK ILP

Individual Unit Learning Plan   Unit:

Name:_____   Block:_____

Learning Style:_____

Indicator(s):

BASELINE ACTIVITIES FOR WHOLE CLASS:

	Activity	Points Earned	Points Possible

Notes:

ASSESSMENT:

	Activity	Points Earned	Points Possible

INDIVIDUAL ACTIVITIES (by learning style): Highlight your choices.			
Visual			
Auditory			
Group Learner			
Kinesthetic			
Expressiveness			
Individual Learner			

SAMPLE ILPS

Individualized Learning Plan by Jane Ku (Elementary Math)

Name:_____   Learning Style:_____

Standard 1: Benchmark 4: Indicator 2e: The student performs this computational procedure: adds and subtracts fractions (like and unlike denominators) greater than or equal to zero (including mixed numbers) without regrouping and without expressing answers in simplest form.

BASELINE ACTIVITIES FOR WHOLE CLASS:

Activity	Points Earned	Points Possible
Teacher reads aloud: *The Hershey's Milk Chocolate Bar Fractions Book* by Jerry Pallotta. All children should have a Hershey's 12-piece chocolate bar to break into pieces when told to do so while book is read. After story, complete short fraction worksheet. Then eat candy!		5
Power Point lesson on finding common denominator. Students take notes in math notebooks.		5
Power Point lesson adding and subtracting fractions. Students work on class worksheet while teacher circulates.		15
Flannel Board presentation on Adding & Subtracting Mixed Numbers. Students work on worksheets with a partner.		15
Play Fraction Jeopardy		5

ASSESSMENTS:

Activity	Points Earned	Points Possible
Poster showing how to add fractions with like denominators		15
Quiz—Adding/Subtracting Fractions with Unlike Denominators		15
Unit Test		50

Scores: _____/45

Assessments: _____/80

Individual Activities: _____/_____

INDIVIDUAL ACTIVITIES (by learning style): Highlight your choices when done.			
Visual	Do problems at http://nlvm.usu.edu/en/nav/frames_asid_106_g_2_t_1.html Harder problems are at http://fen.com/studentactivities/MathSplat/mathsplat.htm (10 points)	Use flash cards to practice finding the least common denominator. [Two fractions are listed on the front of each card and their LCD is on the back.] (7 points)	Use flannel board and fraction pieces to help complete accompanying worksheet on adding & subtracting mixed numbers. (15 points)
Auditory	Listen to the podcast: "Finding a Common Denominator" at http://web.mac.com/stefanhklein/iWeb/Maroon Math/Podcast/716AA880-5A4B-49A3-B5C9-1A6997F25A37.html Complete the accompanying worksheet. (15 points)	Watch video at http://www.glencoe.com/sec/math/msmath/mac04/course1/personal_tutor/personal_tutor.php?t=MAC1_5-5-2 Complete problems on worksheet and color in squares to illustrate. (15 points)	Listen to denominator song at http://web.mac.com/stefanhklein/iWeb/Maroon%20Math/Podcast/BCD726E4-EDEA-4F6B-9393-895AA1CACA2F.html Make a poster showing the 2 ways that the song gives to find a common denominator. (20 points)
Group Learner	Follow the direction sheet to make 5 different colored pizzas, each cut into parts. As a group use the pizza sections to find the answers to worksheet problems. (10 points)	Add or subtract the fractions on the cookie recipe. Use your answers to then make the no-bake cookies! (10 points)	Play Fraction Rummy. Deal cards out to players as directed on the instruction sheet. Make pairs of cards that add up to 1. (7 points)

Kinesthetic	Using the Cuisenaire Rods, complete the accompanying worksheet. (15 points)	Using poker chips and giant circles, place chips in circles to illustrate the mixed number fractions in problems from accompanying worksheet. Complete worksheet. (15 points)	Add fractions with unlike denominators to make pizzas at http://www.mrnussbaum.com/tonyfraction.htm How much money did you make? (10 points)
Expressiveness	Look at "Fraction Riddles" bulletin board. Write 5 of your own fraction riddles. Under each riddle, write the math statement that shows how to get the answer. (20 points)	Write a paragraph telling in detail how to add or subtract fractions that have different denominators. Include at least one example. (15 points)	Create 5 word problems that use fractions and show how to solve them. At least one of your problems should have mixed numbers in it. (20 points)
Individual Learner	Complete the computer lab at http://www.harcourtschool.com/activity/elab2004/gr5/11.html Finish the recording sheet that goes with the lab. (15 points)	Look at example problems on pp. 235 &236 of textbook. Do problems #10–31 on page 237. Student textbook found at http://www.glencoe.com/ose/ Access Code: **F3065EBA48**(20 points)	Do problems at http://www.visualfractions.com/AddUnlike.html Write down your final score. Harder problems are at http://www.jamit.com.au/htmlFolder/app1007.html (10 points)

INDIVIDUALIZED LEARNING PLAN   HS MATH RECOVERY LAB I
(*Created by Bill Brunz*)

Name(s):_____

Learning Style(s):_____

- Objective: The student will determine solution(s) to equations.
- Alg/Geo 1 Unit—Essential Skill: Unit 2 (2.8), E.S. 62–67 (Solve equations)
- GLE: Level 9, Algebra C-3

ACTIVITIES FOR WHOLE CLASS/LAB GROUP:

	Activity	Points Earned	Points Possible
	explorelearning.com, Gizmo: Solving Two Step Equations		100-Gizmo score, 20 each on Gizmo Quiz (80)
	Hollywood Squares PPt. (1-step, 2-Step Rounds)		100-attached Wksht (+20 for tic-tac-toe Win)

Notes:

ASSESSMENT:

	Activity	Points Earned	Points Possible
	One Step-Two Step Test (25) (Can be taken online)		100 (50 Sudden Death Bonus)
	Bingo PPt. Lesson 2.4		100 Equation Card (5-Bingo)
Objectives Accomplished: More Activities needed with:			

INDIVIDUAL ACTIVITIES (by learning style): Circle your choices.		
Note: All activities are 50 daily points, Must do at least 2 activities		
Visual	Go to this site http://www.brainpop.com/math/algebra/equationswithvariables/preview.weml And view movie. Be sure and write down equations shown in the movie and do the quiz at the end of the movie.	Complete Exploration Guide and drawings at Modeling One-Step Equations—Activity B Gizmo | ExploreLearning Must have 25 equations.	http://streaming.discoveryeducation.com/search/assetDetail.cfm?guidAssetID=BFFCB50A-2BC4-4EB2-9B3D-B9E8478F99AA Do quiz at end of movie
Auditory	http://streaming.discoveryeducation.com/search/assetDetail.cfm?guidAssetID=CB1C04F6-AB2E-4EDA-832E-E2939FDF9886 Do quiz at end of movie.	Access site: Play http://www.bbc.co.uk/education/mathsfile/shockwave/games/equationmatch.html up to level three. Show 2 sets of equation matches at each level.	http://streaming.discoveryeducation.com/search/assetDetail.cfm?guidAssetID=B097AF93-C1AD-454F-BAA2-18122AE994DD Do quiz at end of movie.
Group Learner	Choose a partner and challenge another team in equation Jeopardy at http://www.slideshare.net/kwest/two-step-equations-jeopardy Submit all equations solved for credit.	Access the balance site: http://illuminations.nctm.org/ActivityDetail.aspx?id=33 ite Do screen shots of at least 20 equations designed and solved with the applet.	http://www.sheppardsoftware.com/mathgames/Numberballs_algebra_I/numberballsAlgebraI.htm This activity is a partner challenge. Access the site. Challenge your partner to best five of seven games ranking equations against time.

Kinesthetic	Use modeling Gizmo at Modeling Two-Step Equations Gizmo | ExploreLearning With Algebra Tiles for 20 equations. Complete model Drawings	You are going to design a set of Web posters at http:// poster.4teachers.org/ Your poster site should have step-by-step methods of solving 10 equations	This project is a partner activity. http://illuminations. nctm.org/ActivityDetail. aspx?id=33 ite Using the balance scale applet at the above site. Prepare a video presentation for the class using the balance scale and models in the lab. The presentation must show how to solve one and two-step equations with all four arithmetic operators.
Expressiveness	Write a set of 25 one and two-step equations with solutions. Must have 5 categories with 5 levels to use in Jeopardy format.	Access http://mathdl.maa. org/convergence/1/ Find at least 10 problems that require an equation model. Design a PowerPoint of problems.	
Individual Learner	Access http://math.com/ school/subject2/lessons/ S2U3L1GL.html#sm1 Review tutorial on three equation sets. Do online quiz at the end of tutorial and print results.	Access site and play game until reaching level two on 2-step equations game. Print screen to verify level. http://www.what2learn. com/examgames/maths/ equations1/	Complete Gizmo Exploration Guide with Modeling and Solving Two-Step Equations Gizmo | ExploreLearning Do Gizmo Worksheet of 10 equations.

INDIVIDUAL UNIT LEARNING PLAN   UNIT: PROBABILITY AND ODDS
(*Created by Robin Lerner*)

Name:_____ Hour:_____ Date:_____

Learning Styles:_____

Indicator(s): 4.1.K3: The student will be able to explain probability and odds and compute one given the other.

BASELINE ACTIVITIES FOR WHOLE CLASS:

	Activity	Points Earned	Points Possible
	Play Remove One game as class.		5
	Play SPADES game as class.		5
	Skittles Investigation		15

ASSESSMENT:

	Activity	Points Earned	Points Possible
	Interactive Review Quiz http://www.glencoe.com/sec/math/studytools/cgi-bin/msgQuiz.php4?isbn=0-07-829631-5&chapter=11&headerFile=4&state=ks		20
	Test Chapter 2.5–2.6		300

Unit Scores:

    Baseline Activities: _____/_____ pts. _____ %

    Individual Activities: _____/_____ pts. _____ %

    Assessment: _____/_____ pts. _____ %

	INDIVIDUAL ACTIVITIES (by learning style): Highlight your choices.	
Visual	View "Discovering Math: Probability" segment on Probability and Events. Complete worksheet: Probability and Events Level 3 (10 points)	Visit sites on brainpop.com and complete pop quizzes. Record scores here. (10 points)
Auditory	Probability and Odds Video www.unitedstreaming.com	www.brainpop.com/math/dataanalysisandprobability/basicprobability/ www.brainpop.com/math/dataanalysisandprobability/probabilityofindependentevents/
Group Learner	Create spinner games that meet the requirements in the Spinner Info Sheet. (10 points)	Write and perform a skit about probability and odds. See Skit Guidelines. (10 points)
Kinesthetic	Probability and Odds Poster Include indicator specifications. (20 points)	Make a set of at least 25 flashcards that give practice finding probability and odds and one given the other. (10 points)
Expressiveness	Write 5 word problems that would involve probability and/or odds. (10 points)	Write a rap or song to a known tune that explains the difference between probability and odds. (10 points)
Individual Learner	Complete worksheets: Determining Probability Theoretically Level1, Measuring Probability Level 3, and Probability and Events Level 3 (10 points)	Write a journal entry that explains the difficulty some students might have finding probability and odds. (10 points)

10TH GRADE: INDIVIDUAL UNIT LEARNING PLAN

(Created by Jeanna Scheve, 2007)　　　　　Unit: <u>Geologic Time</u>

Indicator(s): <u>4.2.1</u>

Name:_____ Block:_____

Learning Style:_____

BASELINE ACTIVITIES FOR WHOLE CLASS:

	Activity	Points Earned	Points Possible
	Questionnaire		20
	Geologic Basics Video		22
	4.2.1 PPT		10
	Making a Time Line Activity & Show Your Findings wksht.		20
	Geologic Time Web Activity		20

ASSESSMENT:

	Activity	Points Earned	Points Possible
	Clicker Review		20
	Practice Test: http://highered.mcgraw-hill.com/ sites/0078617006/student_view0/unit4/chapter14/standardized_test_practice.html		20
	Geology Indicator Test		

Unit Scores:

　　　Baseline Activities:　　　　_____ / 92　pts.

　　　Individual Activities:　　　　_____ /　pts.

　　　Assessment:　　　　_____ / 40　pts.

INDIVIDUAL ACTIVITIES (by learning style): Highlight your choices.		
Visual	**Tour through the Laws (20)** http://faculty.icc.edu/easc111lab/labs/labf/prelab_f.htm (see cart)	**Photos of the Grand Canyon (20)** http://www.und.nodak.edu/instruct/mineral/101intro/grandcanyon/pics.htm (see cart)
Auditory	**Earth Science: History of the Earth (20) (20:00)** Videos are on the server in the handout folder. (see cart)	**Basics of Geology: Formations of Continents and Mountains (20) (25:43)** Videos are on the server in the handout folder. (see cart)
Group Learner	**Laws of Geology Analogy Poster (20)** Use: http://faculty.icc.edu/easc111lab/labs/labf/prelab_f.htm (see cart)	**Deep Time** Use this site: http://www.pbs.org/wgbh/evolution/change/deeptime/index.html (see cart)
Kinesthetic	**Interpreting Cores to Understand Stratigraphy (20)** (see cart)	**Frosty the Snowman Meets his Demise! (Carbon dating activity) (20)** Use this site as a resource - http://www.bbc.co.uk/history/archaeology/excavations_techniques/carbon_dating.shtml (see cart)
Expressiveness	**The Life Story of a Fossil (20)** Go to: http://www.paleoportal.org/ Click on Site Tour. (see cart)	**Personal Time Line (20)** Use pictures of you & significant events from your life to fill in a personal timeline. (see cart)
Individual Learner	**Geologic Time & Football Wksht. (30)** Use this site: http://pubs.usgs.gov/gip/fossils/numeric.html (see cart)	**Relative vs. Absolute Time (10)** (see cart)

10TH GRADE: INDIVIDUAL LEARNING PLAN

(Created by Jeanna Scheve, 2007)   Unit: 4—Photosynthesis & Respiration

Indicators: 3:5.2 & 3:5.3

Name:_____   Block:_____

Learning Style:_____

BASELINE ACTIVITIES:

Date	Activity	Points Earned	Points Possible
	Photosynthesis & Respiration Overview PPT		10
	United Streaming Video: Energy & Chemistry of Life		20
	Photosynthesis & Cellular Respiration Lab		20
	Concept Review Wksht.		10

Notes:

ASSESSMENTS:

	Activity	Points Earned	Points Possible
	Clicker Review		10
	Jeopardy Review Game: Located on Groups —Scheve-Handout		10
	Photosynthesis & Respiration Indicator Test		Based on %

Baseline: _____ / 60

Individual Activities: _____/_____

Assessments: _____ / 20

Auditory (Please pay close attention to the name of the video!)	Visual
Photosynthesis & Respiration (15): http://glencoe.mcgraw-hill.com/sites/0078617022/student_view0/brainpop_movies.html# After movie, take the quiz.	Internet Activity (30) (see cart)
United Streaming (20) The Flow of Matter & Energy in the Living World: Photosynthesis & Respiration This is on the Groups server for you already pre-loaded. (see cart)	Cell Respiration Animation (10): http://glencoe.mcgraw-hill.com/sites/0078617022/student_view0/unit2/chapter11/concept_animations.html Use a graphic organizer to detail the steps of this process.
Q & A with a partner (30): Obtain an envelope from the cart. Ask your partner 30 cards and then switch roles. Keep a tally of your score.	**Photosynthesis Tutorial (20):** http://www.phschool.com/science/biology_place/biocoach/photosynth/intro.htmlGo through the Introduction, Concepts 1, 4, & 6 only, then take the self-quiz.
	Plant Processes Crossword (10): http://glencoe.mcgraw-hill.com/sites/0078617022/student_view0/unit2/chapter11/interactive_tutor.html

Individual Learner	Expressiveness	Kinesthetic	Group Learner
Rags to Riches! (15): http://www.quia.com/rr/34827.html	Leaf Transpiration Lab (30): Conduct the experiment and then show what happened in your experiment by creating a cartoon about it using Microsoft Word & online clipart!	**Photosynthesis/Respiration Poster (20):** (Limit groups to 3) (see cart)	
BSCS Blue Version (20): p. 178-179 (1-9) & Key Concepts	Photo/Resp. Brochure (20) (see cart)	Rate of Photosynthesis Lab (20) (see cart)	Photosynthesis CD (10): Do Tutorials 1, 5–7, show teacher "end of tutorial" screen and then post-test scores.
Photo/Resp. Sample Quiz (30): http://www.quia.com/quiz/221191.html	**Create a Jeopardy or Millionaire game (20):** reviewing the processes of photosynthesis and respiration. (see cart)	**Do Plants Consume or Release CO2? Or both? (20)** (see cart)	**Respiration Tutorial (30):** http://www.phschool.com/science/biology_place/biocoach/cellresp/intro.html Go through concepts 1–6 and then do the self quiz. Show teacher your score.
		Matching Game (10): http://www.quia.com/mc/318499.html	**Concentration Game (10):** http://glencoe.mcgraw-hill.com/sites/0078664276/student_view0/unit1/chapter5/interactive_tutor.html

INDIVIDUAL UNIT LEARNING PLAN

(Created by Christina Hauer)   Unit: Matter

Name:_____ Class Period:_____

Learning Style:_____

TEKS:

   (A) investigate and identify properties of fluids including density, viscosity, and
        buoyancy;
   (D) relate the chemical behavior of an element including bonding, to its place-
        ment on the periodic table; and
   (E) classify samples of matter from everyday life as being elements, compounds,
        or mixtures.

BASELINE ACTIVITIES FOR WHOLE CLASS:

	Activity	Points Earned	Points Possible
	Matter PPT 16.1		10
	Matter PPT 16.2		10
	Matter PPT 16.3		10

Notes:

ASSESSMENT:

	Activity	Points Earned	Points Possible
	Glencoe.com interactive quiz		20
	Matter Assessment		30

INDIVIDUAL ACTIVITIES (by learning style): Highlight your choices.			
Visual	Physical Science: States of Matterunitedstreaming.com Type title in search boxSummarize video using key word from TEKS(20 points)	Properties and Changes of Matter Interactive Quiz http://glencoe.mcgraw-hill.com/sites/007877846x/student_view0/unit2/chapter5/section_1_self-check_quiz-eng_.html(10 points)	**Experiment! Classifying Bonds Activity See tray (15 points)**
Auditory	Physical Science Series: Chemical Bondingunitedstreaming.com Type title in search box Pretest and video quiz(20 points)	**Measuring Matter Brain POP Movie** http://glencoe.mcgraw-hill.com/sites/007877846x/student_view0/brainpop_movies.html#select Measuring Matter and carry out the quiz at the end and show score to teacher(15 points)	**Partner Question and Answer PracticeFlashcards are located in trayQuiz each other over the terms until at least ten terms as quizzed by teacher.(15 points)**

Group Learner	**How are the mass and volume of a substance related?** **Mini Lab** **See tray** **(25 points)**	Web Quest Phytochemicals and a Healthy Diet http://glencoe.mcgraw-hill.com/sites/007877846x/student_view0/unit2/webquest.html Fill in data table, questions and conclusion (**30 points**)	**Buoyant Boat Activity** http://www.sciencenetlinks.com/lessons.cfm?DocID=143 **See tray (25 points)**
Kinesthetic	**What's that liquid?** **Determining Density and Analyzing Data** **(30 points)**	**Viscosity Tube Activity** **See tray (25 points)** **Kinetic Theory Quick Activity See tray (10 points)**	
Expressiveness	**Classification of Matter Poster—See expressiveness tray for rubric (25 points)**	**Write a song or poem that incorporates the TEKS** **See tray for rubric** **(25 points)**	**Block Activity** **See tray (15 pts.)**
Individual Learner	**Chapter 16 Review Pg. 279** **Vocabulary Review** **Concept Review** **Problems (23 points)**	**Interactive Math Practice** http://glencoe.mcgraw-hill.com/sites/007877846x/student_view0/unit2/chapter5/math_practice.htmlshow your calculations on a separate sheet of paper (20 points)	**Discussion Questions** **See tray (14 points)**

SAMPLE OF Y!C STRATEGY STUDENT FEEDBACK SURVEYS

(This survey was created using a free trial on surveymonkey.com in the spring of 2008 by Jeanna Scheve, Anderson County High School, in Garnett, KS.)

Question	Possible Responses Listed
1. Are you male or female?	Male, Female
2. What is your grade level?	9th, 10th, 11th, 12th
3. Activities in class were appropriate for my learning styles.	Yes, No
4. Individual work activities deepened my understanding of the topics being learned?	Yes, No
5. Using learning styles to customize my education was beneficial for me.	Yes, No
6. Knowing how I learned material best helped me in other classes.	Yes, No
7. I prefer having choices in how I learn the topic presented versus conventional learning methods (notes, lectures, tests, etc.)	Yes, No
8. Using learning styles to customize my learning led me to be better prepared for the science assessment and to approach the assessment more positively and motivated.	Yes, No
9. If I could change one thing about the learning plans, it would be:	(Comment field inserted for students to write.)
10. My favorite individual learning activities were:	(Comment field inserted for students to write.)

Of course, various questions can be asked on a student survey depending on what the teacher feels is necessary information to guide their practice. Do not shy away from gathering student opinions! They can help you to see a new perspective and enhance the working relationship between you and your students!

RESULTS OF Y!C STRATEGY STUDENT FEEDBACK SURVEY

(These are the results from the survey sample on the previous page that were gathered in the spring of 2008. Some students (depending on their age) had been involved with Y!C since 2004. Comments for questions 9 & 10 can be found in the Student Testimonial section of this manual.)

Question	Student Answer
1. Are you male or female?	Male – 45%, Female – 54.9%
2. What is your grade level?	9th – 0% 11th – 40.8% 10th – 26.8% 12th – 32.4%
3. Activities in class were appropriate for my learning styles.	**Yes – 95.8%** No – 4.2%
4. Individual work activities deepened my understanding of the topics being learned?	**Yes – 87.7%** No – 12.3%
5. Using learning styles to customize my education was beneficial for me?	**Yes – 82.4%** No – 17.6%
6. Knowing how I learned material best helped me in other classes.	**Yes – 63.0%** No – 37.0%
7. I prefer having choices in how I learn the topic presented versus conventional learning methods (notes, lectures, tests, etc.)	**Yes – 93.1%** No – 6.9%
8. Using learning styles to customize my learning lead me to be better prepared for the science assessment and to approach the assessment more positively and motivated?	**Yes – 69.0%** No – 31.0%

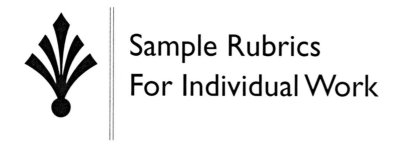

Sample Rubrics
For Individual Work

"He who is afraid of asking is ashamed of learning."
—Danish Proverb

PRAIRIE BROCHURE RUBRIC

PROJECT REQUIREMENTS:

Information Needed

_____/4 **Names** of students, illustration of species, common name of species, and scientific name of species.

_____/3 **Define** a prairie ecosystem, and **list** the basic environmental conditions and climate of the Great Plains.

_____/6 **Description** of _at least three_ **physical adaptations** AND **detailed explanation** of how each characteristic makes the species well adapted to the prairie environment.

_____/6 **Description** of _at least three_ **behavioral adaptations** AND **detailed explanation** of how each characteristic makes the species well adapted to the prairie environment.

_____/3 **Description** of changes that may occur in this ecosystem if this organism were to become extinct.

_____/3 **Bibliography** of resources used (at least three different resources must be used for this brochure)

OTHER:

_____/3 **Resources** are listed correctly (Web site address, name of article used, year of book, etc.)

_____/1 **Neatness**

_____/1 **Creativity**

____-_____ Use of correct **grammar and spelling**. (1 point deduction per error.)

_____/30 **POINTS TOTAL**

VIRUSES & BACTERIA POSTER

Content:
1. Ways a virus enters the body.
2. How a virus attacks the cells and replicates
3. How the body responds to the attack

Neatness & Organization
1. Use of color
2. Words neat, legible, and appropriate size
3. Diagrams/pictures accurate
4. Title

Vocabulary:
1. Vector
2. White Blood Cell
3. Phagocytosis
4. Immune Response
5. B-cell
6. Memory Cell
7. Immunity

	5	3	1
Content	All required information is accurate and embellished by other appropriate information.	All required information is accurate.	Includes all required information.
Vocabulary	All vocabulary words defined correctly and used in context within the content of the poster.	All vocabulary words defined correctly.	Vocabulary words visible.
Neatness & Organization	Poster is organized to enhance the ease of reading, it uses color appropriately, words enhance the meaning of pictures/graphics.	Poster uses color appropriately, both words and graphics are used.	Legible with little or no use of color. Organization is jumbled with no specific direction.

MULTIMEDIA PROJECT: POWERPOINT

Teacher name: _____   Student Name: _____

CATEGORY	4	3	2	1
Attractiveness	Makes excellent use of font, color, graphics, effects, etc., to enhance the presentation.	Makes good use of font, color, graphics, effects, etc., to enhance to presentation.	Makes use of font, color, graphics, effects, etc., but occasionally these detract from the presentation content.	Use of font, color, graphics, effects, etc., but these often distract from the presentation content.
Presentation	Well-rehearsed with smooth delivery that holds audience attention.	Rehearsed with fairly smooth delivery that holds audience attention most of the time.	Delivery not smooth, but able to maintain interest of the audience most of the time.	Delivery not smooth and audience attention often lost.
Requirements	All requirements are met and exceeded.	All requirements are met.	One requirement was not completely met.	More than one requirement was not completely met.
Mechanics	No misspellings or grammatical errors.	Three or fewer misspellings and/or mechanical errors.	Four misspellings and/or grammatical errors.	More than 4 errors in spelling or grammar.
Content	Covers topic in-depth with details and examples. Subject knowledge is excellent.	Includes essential knowledge about the topic. Subject knowledge appears to be good.	Includes essential information about the topic but there are 1-2 factual errors.	Content is minimal OR there are several factual errors.

Attractiveness: _____

Presentation: _____

Requirements: _____

Mechanics: _____

Content: _____

TOTAL: _____ **out of 20** _____

USD #365					
Poem Rubric					
Name:			**Teacher:**		
Date Submitted:			**Title of Work:**		
	Criteria				**Points**
	1	**2**	**3**	**4**	
Organization	Sequence of information is difficult to follow.	Reader has difficulty following work because student jumps around.	Student presents information in logical sequence which reader can follow.	Information in logical, interesting sequence which reader can follow.	
Content Knowledge	Student does not have grasp of information; student cannot answer questions about subject.	Student is uncomfortable with content and is able to demonstrate basic concepts.	Student is at ease with content, but fails to elaborate.	Student demonstrates full knowledge (more than required).	
Grammar and Spelling	Work has four or more spelling errors and/or grammatical errors.	Presentation has three misspellings and/or grammatical errors.	Presentation has no more than two misspellings and/or grammatical errors.	Presentation has no misspellings or grammatical errors.	
Neatness	Work is illegible.	Work has three or four areas that are sloppy.	Work has one or two areas that are sloppy.	Work is neatly done.	
References	Work displays no references.	Work does not have the appropriate number of required references.	Reference section was completed incorrectly	Work displays the correct number of references, written correctly.	
				Total --->	

SOURCES

Bess, James (1997). *Teaching Well and Liking it: Motivating Faculty to Teach Effectively.* Baltimore, MD: The Johns Hopkins University Press.

Brandt, Ronald (1998). *Powerful Learning.* Alexandria, VA: ASCD.

Clarke & Frazer (2003). Making Learning Personal: Educational Practices that Work. In J. DiMartino, J. Clarke, & D. Wolk (Eds.), *Personalized Learning: Preparing High School Students to Create Their Futures* (pp.174–193). Lanham, MD: Scarecrow Press.

Devaney, Laura. *eSchool News,* Sept. 9 2009, "Reinventing Education: As Schools Nationwide Examine New Federal Priorities, San Diego Unveils a Five-Year Plan to Transform the Way Students Are Taught,", http://www.eschoolnews.com/news/special-reports/special-reports-articles/index.cfm?i=60608. Accessed Nov. 3, 2009.

Finkel, Donald L. (1999). Teaching with Your Mouth Shut, Portsmouth, NH: Boynton/Cook Publishers, Inc.

Gardner, Howard. (1983). *Frames of Mind: The Theory of Multiple Intelligences.* New York. Basic Books.

Marzano, Robert J., Pickering, Debra J. and Pollock, Jane E. 2001. *Classroom Instruction that Works.* Alexandria, VA: ASCD

Marzano, Robert J. (2003). *What Works in Schools, Translating Research into Action,* Alexandria, VA: ASCD

Tech & Learning Nov. 3, 2009, "Big Picture: PERSONALIZATION + PORTFOLIOS", http://www.techlearning.com/article/25072. Accessed Nov. 3, 2009.

Tomlinson, Carol Ann. (1999). *The Differentiated Classroom, Responding to the Needs of All Learners,* Alexandria, VA: Association for Supervision and Curriculum and Development

Wormeli, Rick. (2006). *Fair Isn't Always Equal, Assessing and Grading in the Differentiated Classroom,* Portland, ME, Stenhouse Publishers

CONTRIBUTING WRITERS

- Pamela Powell
- Christina Hauer
- Robin Lerner
- Elizabeth Siegel
- Jane Ku
- Bill Brunz

!

FOR INQUIRIES OR TRAINING
ON YES ! CAN FOR YOUR SCHOOL,
PLEASE CONTACT:

Kelli Allen
UTeach
University of Texas at Austin
E-mail: kallen@austin.utexas.edu
Phone: (785) 204-1880

Jeanna Scheve
Anderson County Jr/Sr High School
E-mail: jmscheve@hotmail.com
Phone: (785) 204-2132

Or visit our Web site at:
http://www.yesicanresources.com/

Breinigsville, PA USA
24 August 2010
244101BV00002B/2/P